DATE DUE		
JUL 15 2013		

The Urbana Free Library

To renew: call 217-367-4057
or go to "*urbanafreelibrary.org*"
and select "Renew/Request Items"

CRAFT SKILLS

STEPHANIE TURNBULL

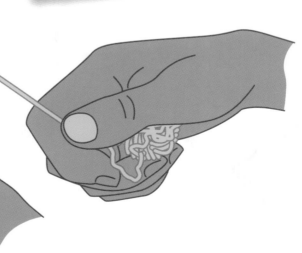

A+
Smart Apple Media

Published by Smart Apple Media, an imprint of Black Rabbit Books
P.O. Box 3263, Mankato, Minnesota 56002
www.blackrabbitbooks.com

Printed in the United States of America at Corporate Graphics, North Mankato, Minnesota.

Library of Congress Cataloging-in-Publication Data

Turnbull, Stephanie.
 Craft skills / Stephanie Turnbull.
    p. cm. — (Super skills)
 Includes index.
 Summary: "Provides readers with step-by-step instructions to create innovative crafts using everyday household items. Outlines Origami, weaving, papier-mâché and many more fun and easy crafts for children of all ages and abilities"—Provided by publisher.
 ISBN 978-1-59920-796-4 (library binding)
 1. Handicraft—Juvenile literature. I. Title.
 TT157.T87 2013
 680--dc23
                                   2011038280

Created by Appleseed Editions, Ltd.
Designed and illustrated by Guy Callaby
Edited by Mary-Jane Wilkins
Photo research by Su Alexander

Picture credits
l = left, r = right, c = center, t = top, b = bottom
Contents page Fotosutra.com/Shutterstock; 4tl Valzan/Shutterstock, tr Hemera Technologies/Thinkstock, bl Originalpunkt/Shutterstock, br HelleM/Shutterstock; 5 Mostovyi Sergii Igorevich/Shutterstock; 6t Thinkstock, b Eric Isselée/Shutterstock; 8t Thinkstock, b Digital Vision/Thinkstock; 10 Hemera Technologies/Thinkstock; 11 Chrisbrignell/Shutterstock; 12 Thinkstock; 13 Stockbyte/Thinkstock; 14 Thinkstock; 15 Photos.com/Thinkstock; 16, 18, 20, 21, & 22t Thinkstock, 22b Design pics/John Kroetch/ Thinkstock; 24t Thinkstock, cl Brand X Pictures/Thinkstock, cr & bl Stephanie Turnbull, br Jupiterimages/Thinkstock; 25, 26, 27, 28 & 29 Thinkstock; 30l Feng Yu/Shutterstock, r Frances L Fruit/Shutterstock; 31 Shutterstock & Thinkstock
Cover: scissors Thinkstock, glue brush Anzhely K/Shutterstock, buttons Garsya/Shutterstock

PO1444
2-2012

9 8 7 6 5 4 3 2 1

CONTENTS

CLEVER CRAFTS

If you're feeling creative and want to make useful or decorative things, there are many craft skills you can learn. This book gives you great ideas for turning materials into models, masks, puppets, games, and more. You can then go on to invent your own brilliant designs!

Think Crafty

You may want to buy some special craft supplies, but there are many everyday things you can use—unusual buttons, scraps of fabric, textured paper, or oddly-shaped containers. Look carefully at things before you throw them away. Could you recycle them as craft materials?

◀ *A set of **watercolor** or **acrylic** paints are useful for many craft projects.*

▲ *Craft supplies like feathers are great for decorating homemade masks.*

SUPER ★ FACTS

★ *The Fabergé company famously crafted lavish jewelry, including jeweled gold and silver eggs. In 2007, a Fabergé egg was sold for over $18 million.*

★ *During Thailand's annual wax festival, artists shape huge, intricate wax models.*

★ *Prehistoric craftspeople made carvings from bones and mammoth tusks.*

Get Organized

Before you start any project, collect all the equipment you need. Make sure you have a big, clear workspace, and lots of time. If you rush something, it won't turn out as neatly or successfully as you wanted. Handle sharp tools carefully, and get adult help when needed. Finally, don't forget to clean up afterwards!

Plan each project before you start cutting and gluing. This will help to avoid wasting materials.

HINTS AND WARNINGS

Boxes with a lightbulb symbol contain handy hints for making your craft projects even better.

Look out for the exclamation marks too—these boxes give safety warnings and other helpful advice.

PAPER PROJECTS

Paper is one of the most basic craft materials, but it's also one of the best. It's cheap to buy, although you may already have plenty at home, for example wrapping paper, newspaper, magazines, and old notepads. See what you can find!

Giftwrap Beads

Here's a quick paper project to get you started. Find a piece of shiny giftwrap and glue it around a drinking straw. When the glue is dry, cut up the straw and thread the pieces onto string or elastic to make jewelry and dangling zipper decorations.

▲ *You can make great cards by cutting and layering paper, especially if you choose contrasting colors and textures.*

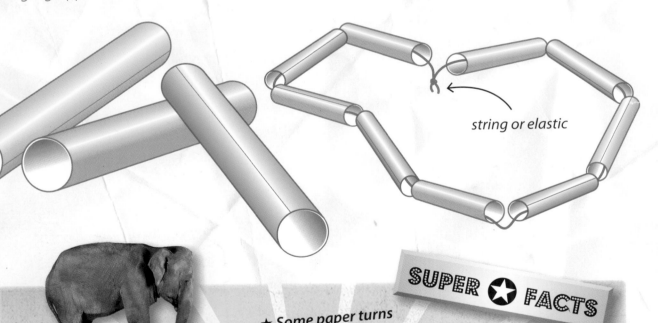

string or elastic

★ *Modern paper is made from **pulped** wood, but cotton, straw, bananas, and even elephant dung can all be used.*

★ *Some paper turns yellow with age because of a chemical called lignin in the wood pulp. More expensive paper has the lignin removed, so it stays white.*

SUPER ★ FACTS

★ *The word paper comes from the Egyptian word papyrus, a type of plant. Ancient Egyptians made paper from strips of papyrus stems.*

Papermaking

Recycle old newspapers to make your own paper. You could also use envelopes or other scrap paper, just make sure it isn't glossy or very thick.

1. Tear sheets of paper into pieces and leave to soak for a few hours or overnight.

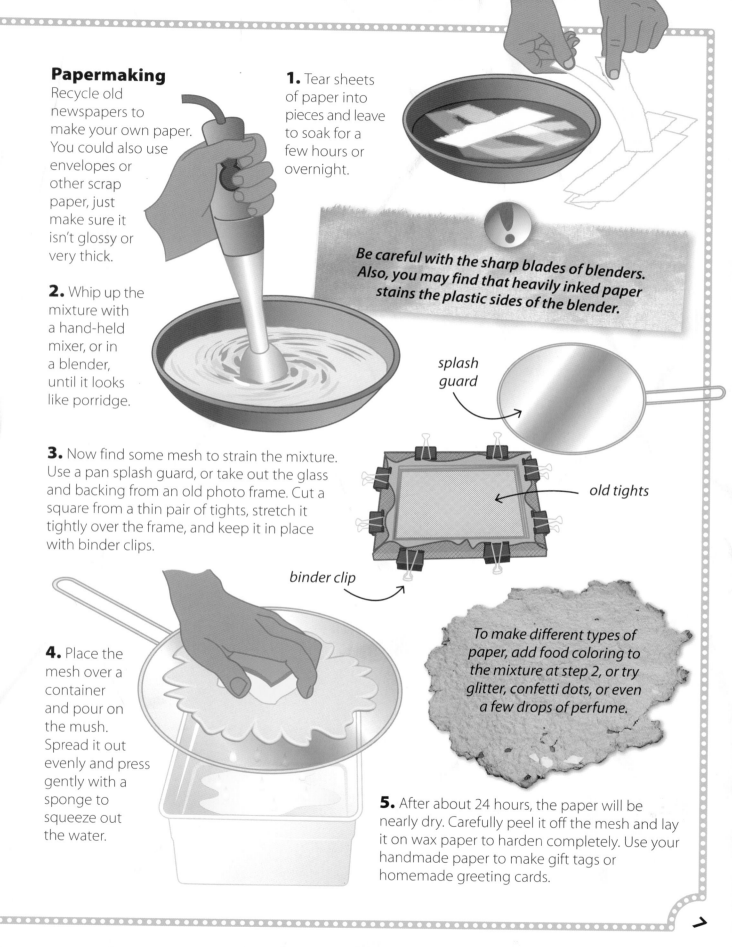

2. Whip up the mixture with a hand-held mixer, or in a blender, until it looks like porridge.

Be careful with the sharp blades of blenders. Also, you may find that heavily inked paper stains the plastic sides of the blender.

splash guard

3. Now find some mesh to strain the mixture. Use a pan splash guard, or take out the glass and backing from an old photo frame. Cut a square from a thin pair of tights, stretch it tightly over the frame, and keep it in place with binder clips.

old tights

binder clip

4. Place the mesh over a container and pour on the mush. Spread it out evenly and press gently with a sponge to squeeze out the water.

To make different types of paper, add food coloring to the mixture at step 2, or try glitter, confetti dots, or even a few drops of perfume.

5. After about 24 hours, the paper will be nearly dry. Carefully peel it off the mesh and lay it on wax paper to harden completely. Use your handmade paper to make gift tags or homemade greeting cards.

ORIGAMI IDEAS

Origami is the Japanese art of folding paper to create models. There is no cutting, sticking, or mess! Experts make intricate sculptures, sometimes using several pieces of paper. Here are two easy origami animals to start with.

Simple Swan

1. Fold a square of paper in half diagonally, then open it out.

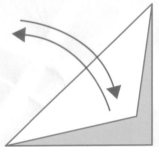

Make the paper about 6 sq. in. (15 sq. cm), or smaller if you prefer.

2. With the center crease vertical, fold each half into the middle to make a kite shape.

3. Turn over the paper and do the same again.

4. Fold the bottom point up to the top point, then fold the top section back down halfway.

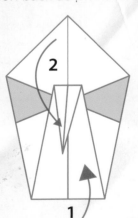

5. Fold the paper in half down the original center crease.

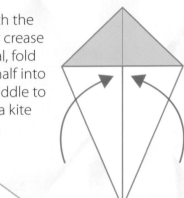

head

neck

wing

6. Lift the neck section and crease it in place, then do the same with the head. Fold down the edges of the flaps at each side to make wings.

Jumping Frog

1. Cut a rectangle about 3x5 in. (7.5x12 cm). Fold the top right corner to the opposite edge, then open it out again.

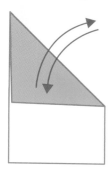

2. Fold the top left corner in the same way and open it out again.

The two creases make an X.

3. Turn over the paper and fold down the top section so the ends of the X meet. Open it out again.

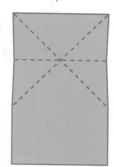

4. Turn over the paper. Push the last crease inwards and down so the top section forms a triangle.

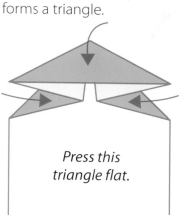

Press this triangle flat.

5. Fold up the corners of the top triangle layer to either side of the center point.

These are the front legs.

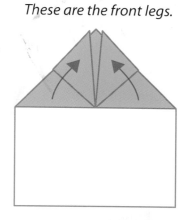

6. Fold the left and right sides to the middle.

7. Fold up the bottom edge to about halfway up the legs, then fold it back down to meet the bottom of the paper.

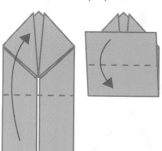

8. Pull out the front legs so the frog can stand, and crease the ends to make feet.

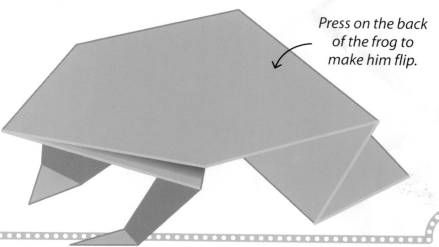

Press on the back of the frog to make him flip.

PAPIER-MÂCHÉ

Papier-mâché (French for "chewed paper") is a cheap and very useful craft material. Here's how to make perfect papier-mâché, and some ideas for fantastic mask designs.

Use a whisk to get rid of lumps.

Prepare Your Paste

First, make your paste. Some people use wallpaper paste and others water down white glue to make it runny. The simplest method is to mix equal amounts of flour and water in a large bowl or plastic container. The mixture should be like thick soup. Add extra water or flour if you think it needs it.

Get Papering!

1. Blow up a balloon to roughly the size of your head. Tape it to a flower pot or bowl to keep it still.

2. Tear a few sheets of newspaper into strips about 1 in. (2.5 cm) wide and 4 in. (10 cm) long.

3. Dip a strip of newspaper into the paste, hold it up and run it through your fingers to squeeze off the extra paste. Lay it flat on the balloon and smooth it down.

4. Add more overlapping strips to cover the front of the balloon.

5. Put a couple more layers on top, then leave to dry overnight. Prop the balloon on its side so the strips don't slide off.

6. Add more layers the next day. (You'll need to make new paste.) Once these have dried, pop the balloon and peel it off the papier-mâché shell.

7. Trim the mask to fit your face. Using nail scissors, carefully cut out eye and mouth holes. Add features like a nose and eyebrows by sticking on scrunched-up newspaper with masking tape and covering them with more papier-mâché.

8. Now paint and decorate your mask.

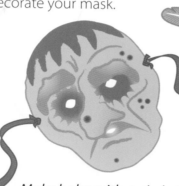

Make holes with a pin in the sides and tie on a length of elastic or two pieces of ribbon so you can wear your mask.

Newsprint often shows under paint, so use white paper for the last layer—then you'll have a plain surface to paint on.

Mask Shapes

Remember that your mask doesn't have to cover your whole face. Cut it just above your nose to make a half mask, or trim it more to make an eye mask. You could decorate it with sequins, beads, and jewels, or paint it to match a superhero costume!

MAKING MODELS

If you want to sculpt your own models, jewelry, or decorations, there are many materials to try. You can use papier-mâché (see pages 10 and 11) or buy different types of clay from craft stores. You can also make your own modeling dough.

Simple Salt Dough

Salt dough is cheap and easy to make, and has been used for modeling since ancient Egyptian times.

1. In a large bowl, mix 1 c (250 mL) flour, ¾ c (180 mL) salt, ½ c (120 mL) warm water, and a 1 tsp (5 mL) of vegetable oil.

2. Make the mixture into a ball with your hands. If it's sticky, add a little flour. If it's too dry, add a few drops of water. Sprinkle flour on your work surface and knead for about five minutes to make a smooth, stretchy dough.

Salt Dough Sculpting

Many people make salt dough Christmas decorations using cookie cutters, but there are lots of other things you can do. Here are a few ideas to get you started.

Make a sign for your bedroom door by rolling out the dough and cutting shapes with a plastic knife or cookie cutters. To stick two pieces together, moisten them with water first.

◄ *Use cookie cutters to make neat shapes and poke a hole in each. When they're hard, paint and thread them to make jewelry.*

Hollow out balls of dough to make bowls or pencil pots, then decorate the sides.

Try modeling fun fake food, for example, fruit, a burger, or a full dinner plate!

Make a hole with a pencil so you can thread ribbon or string through later.

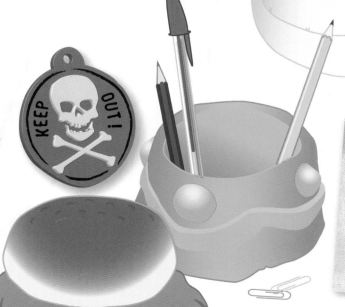

Baking Models

To make the dough set hard, lay your models on a baking sheet and put it in the oven at its lowest setting for about an hour and a half. Turn off the oven afterwards but leave the models inside to cool slowly. Once they're cold, paint them with watercolor or acrylic paints.

Even though the oven isn't hot, use oven mitts and be careful. Ask for help if you need it.

EASY WEAVING

Weaving is an ancient skill used to make baskets, rugs, and tapestries. The basic technique is very simple—the key is to find interesting things to weave with. Why not try cutting long strips from old clothes, glossy magazine pages, or even colorful plastic bags?

▲ *Woven material has two sets of threads: one going across and the other down.*

How to Weave

1. First, glue lots of strips to one horizontal strip, like this. Stick one underneath, the next on top and so on.

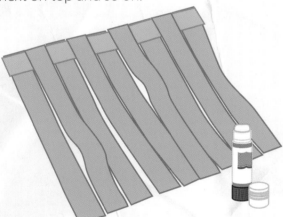

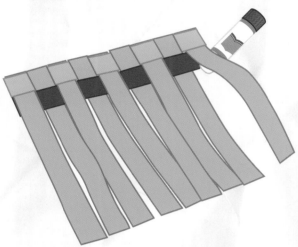

2. Now thread a strip through the vertical strips, going under the first, over the next and so on. Glue it in place at each end.

3. Do the same with another strip, but start by going over the first vertical strip. Add more alternating strips until you've filled the frame.

Your woven square could be a place mat, a flag, or the decoration on a greeting card.

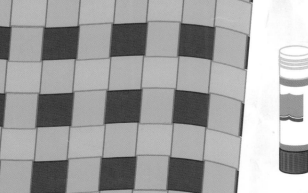

Straw Loom Weaving

Here's an easy way of making your own **loom** for weaving yarn.

1. Find four drinking straws. Thread a piece of yarn through each, like this.

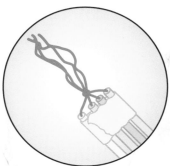

2. Tie the pieces of yarn together at the top and push the straws up to the knot. Stick masking tape around the top of the straws.

3. Tie the end of a ball of yarn around the first straw, then weave the yarn under the second straw, over the third and under the fourth.

4. Now go back over the fourth straw, under the third and so on. Weave lots of rows, pushing the yarn up as you go to keep the rows close together.

5. To switch colors, tie the yarn around an outside straw and cut the end. Start a new color as in step 3, tucking the loose ends of yarn inside the weaving.

6. When you reach the end of the straws, tie the yarn to an outside straw and cut it. Remove the masking tape and carefully pull out the straws, one at a time.

7. Push the weaving up to the knot, tie another knot at the bottom, and trim the loose ends. Your woven strip makes a perfect bookmark.

★ The world's largest handmade woven carpet is as big as a soccer field. It was made to fit inside an enormous mosque in Iran.

▼ *This is a hand-woven Navajo blanket.*

SUPER ★ FACTS

★ The Native American Navajo people are famous for weaving colorful rugs and blankets with bold patterns.

WOOLY MONSTERS

Why not turn yarn into pom-poms? These fluffy balls can be any size or color, and are perfect for creating hanging decorations, furry animals, or perhaps a whole alien invasion of not-very-scary wooly monsters!

Pom-Pom Rings

Find a piece of cardboard and draw around a glass or round lid. Cut it out, then make another circle in the middle by drawing around a coin or smaller lid. Cut this out, too, then draw around your doughnut shape to make another identical ring. Put the two together.

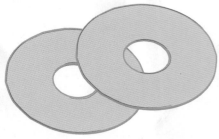

The smaller hole should be about a third as wide as the ring.

The bigger the hole in the middle, the longer your pom-pom will take to make.

Crazy Creatures

1. Start winding a long length of yarn around the rings like this. Don't worry about tying the loose end—leave it hanging over the edge.

2. Keep winding. When you come to the end of the yarn, leave the end hanging and start a new length as before. Keep going until the hole is filled.

When the hole is tiny, use a thick needle to pull the yarn through.

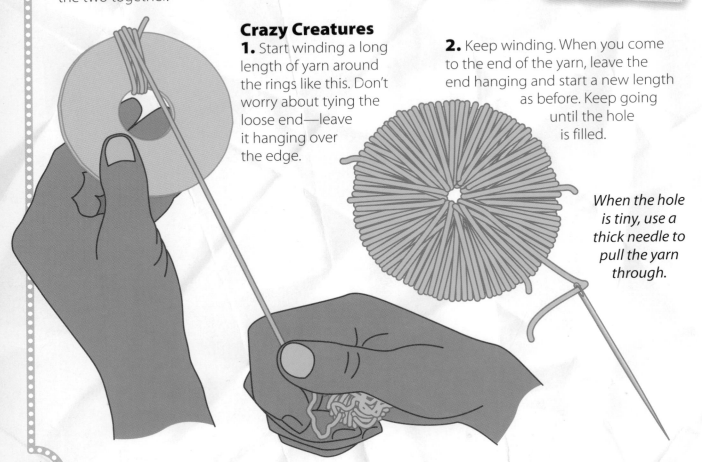

3. Carefully snip around the edge of the circle with sharp scissors, pushing one blade between the two rings.

4. Pull a length of yarn between the rings and tie it tightly, then tear off the rings.

5. Fluff up the pom-pom and trim any longer ends. This is the alien's body.

6. Cut a smaller set of rings and make a second pom-pom for the alien's head. Stick it on the body with a blob of white glue.

hand soap bottle top

paper clips

7. Cut a base from a piece of card and glue your alien to it. Make arms and legs from pipe cleaners, then add other features using buttons, bottle tops, paper clips, card, **felt**, or any other craft supplies you can find.

Use your imagination—and lots of colored pom-poms—to create a swarm of strange wooly space visitors!

rubber tap washers

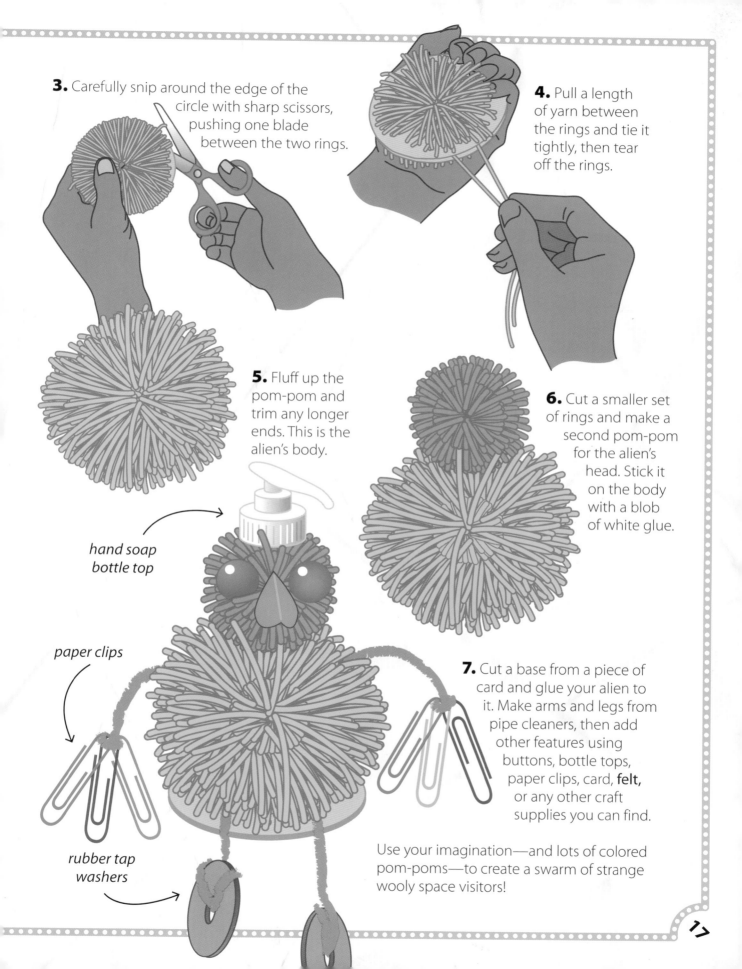

17

PUPPETS

Puppets can be **marionettes** with strings, finger and glove puppets, or models with mechanical moving parts. Here are two hand puppet designs you can adapt to make other characters. The more imaginative you are, the more personality your puppet will have!

Felt is useful as it doesn't fray. Fasten the safety pins inside the sock.

Silly Sock Dog

For a funny long-nosed dog, stuff the toe of an old sock with cotton balls or scraps of material. Your thumb goes in the heel to make the mouth.

Cut big eyes, floppy ears, and a long tongue from felt or paper, and fix them in place with glue or safety pins. Before you add each one, put your hand in the sock and mark its position.

Billy Big Mouth

Is this a fearsome dragon, a toothy crocodile, or a mad monster? You decide.

1. Cut off the flaps of an egg carton and separate the two halves. Paint the inside and let it dry.

2. Tape the halves together at one end, then stick a strip of card stock on each half to make finger bands.

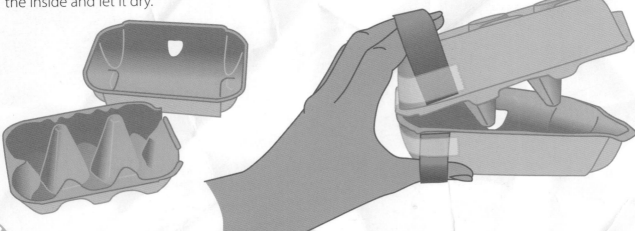

3. Cut one leg from an old pair of leggings, or a sleeve from an old sweater. Pull it over the egg carton, then cut along the sides to make the mouth.

The rest of the material will cover your arm.

4. Stretch the cut edges over the carton and carefully staple or glue them in place.

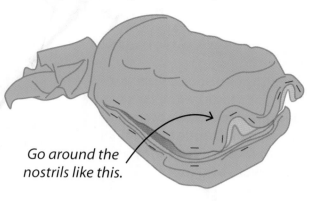

Go around the nostrils like this.

5. Make eyes by sticking scrunched-up tissue inside plastic lids, then gluing them to the material. Stick googly eyes on top. Add a tongue and other decorations.

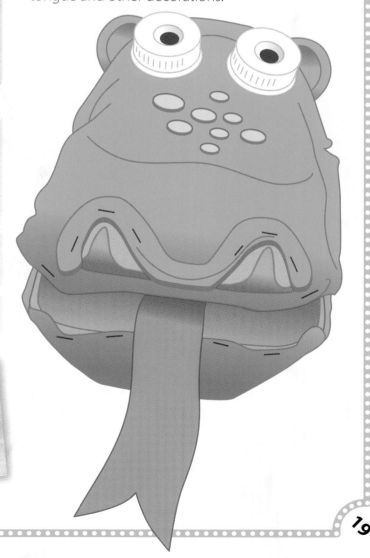

SUPER ★ FACTS

★ **Punch and Judy are famous European hand puppets. Punch has a squawky voice made by a device called a swazzle in the puppeteer's mouth.**

★ **Ancient Chinese people invented shadow puppets. These are flat figures, moved by rods and lit from behind, so they cast shadows on a screen.**

★ **In Vietnam, you can see water puppet plays. Puppets operated by rods and strings dip, glide, and dance in a large pool of water.**

Try making puppets using other craft skills, such as papier-mâché (page 10), salt dough (page 12), and pom-poms (page 16).

TOYS AND GAMES

Designing your own toys and games is fun. You could try sticking a magazine picture on to cardboard and cutting it into jigsaw pieces, or creating a board game with salt dough. Here are some more great ideas.

◀ *This jigsaw puzzle is made of wood, but you could design a similar one using thick cardboard.*

Speedy Spinner

This paper toy has propellers that whiz around like helicopter blades.

1. Draw this shape on paper and cut it out. Paint one side with watercolors, let it dry, then turn it over and paint the other side. You could also sprinkle on glitter while the paint is wet.

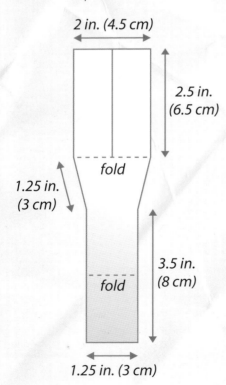

2 in. (4.5 cm)

2.5 in. (6.5 cm)

fold

1.25 in. (3 cm)

3.5 in. (8 cm)

fold

1.25 in. (3 cm)

2. When it's dry, fold up the bottom section and hold it in place with two paper clips. Bend the two propellers backwards and forwards a few times until they're floppy, then flip one forwards and one backwards.

3. Let your spinner drop from somewhere high, and watch it spin!

Try racing several spinners with friends.

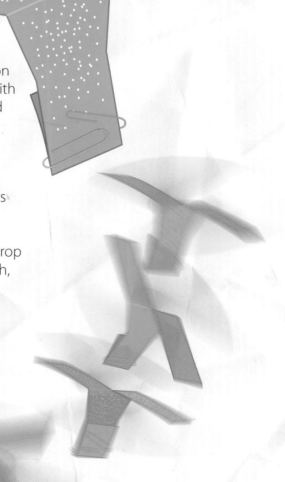

Marble Maze

Make this bendy straw maze as tricky as you like—just be sure the gaps are wide enough for a marble to roll through.

1. Find a sturdy cardboard lid, for example from a shoe box, and paint the inside.

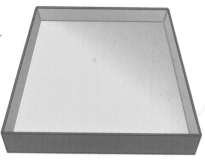

2. Design a maze on tracing paper the same size as the lid. Do this by dividing the paper into squares.

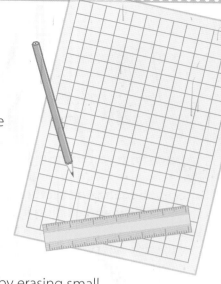

3. Next, make a way to the center by erasing small sections. Make more gaps to create other routes, but make sure they don't reach the center.

4. Trace over the other side of the maze in pencil, then position it on the lid and go over it again to transfer the pencil marks to the cardboard. Carefully cut a hole in the center of the maze with sharp scissors or a craft knife, plus a gap at the start.

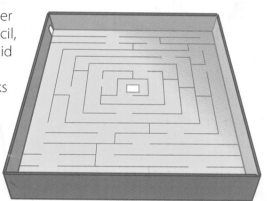

5. On the back, tape a square of net (cut from a fruit bag) over the hole to stop your marble rolling away when you finish the maze.

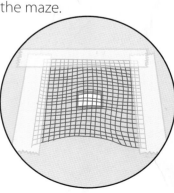

6. Cut straws to match the maze walls, using the bendy pieces for corners. Stick them in place with a glue stick. When the glue is dry, your puzzle is ready.

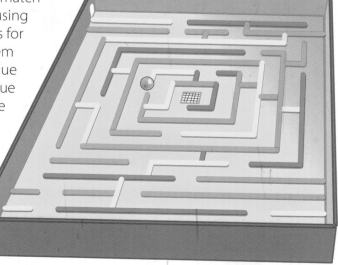

FUN WITH FOOD

You can have some inventive craft fun with food. Using just a knife, a cutting board, and lots of imagination, fruits and vegetables can become funny faces or bizarre animals. Once you've photographed your creations, you can eat them!

Fresh Supplies

The best way to get started on food sculpture is to open the fridge or head to the supermarket. Study items carefully. What do they look like? What could you turn them into? One essential supply is a bag of black-eyed peas. They make perfect eyes!

black-eyed peas

Take care when using a knife. Don't rush, and make sure your fingers don't get in the way!

Silly Faces

Any rounded fruit or vegetable can become a head, with the end of the core as a nose. Apples, oranges, kiwis, and peppers are good to start with. Buy some of each, so you can experiment with facial expressions.

Decide where you want the eyes. Cut small holes in the skin or peel, and press in black-eyed peas.

Carefully cut a mouth. Push in sunflower seeds for teeth and add a sliver of carrot for a tongue —or use your own ideas!

Green onions make good heads because of the sprouting "hair." Dip a toothpick in blue or green food dye and poke two eyes. Cut a mouth with a knife and add red food dye with the other end of the toothpick.

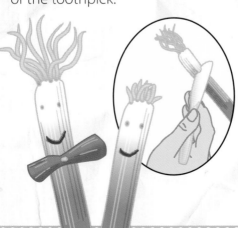

Pieces of uncooked spaghetti make great spiky hair.

Crazy Critters

To make whole animals, try using foods that are body-shaped, such as potatoes or avocados, and add limbs by sticking toothpicks into other, smaller fruits or vegetables. You can also cut out wings or arms with a knife. Here's an easy penguin to try.

1. Cut off the end of an eggplant so it stands on a cutting board.

2. Carefully slice downwards to make the penguin's white front, and make cuts for his wings. Make eye holes and push in black-eyed peas.

3. Create an Antarctic scene with several penguins on a white backdrop. Use the cut eggplant ends to make seal heads popping out of the water!

NATURE CRAFTS

How about looking in the garden for craft materials? You could weave with long grasses, make animals from pine cones and sticks, or glue feathers and bark onto masks. Here are some ideas for using stones and flowers.

Pebble Letters

Don't stick ordinary letter magnets on your fridge —use painted pebbles instead! They're fun to make and look a lot more attractive than the plastic ones.

▲ *Autumn is a great time to collect seed heads, nut shells, and other interesting natural craft materials.*

1. Collect lots of small pebbles that are fairly flat. Clean them and let them dry.

2. Paint the pebbles with acrylic paint. Leave them to dry, then use a thin brush to paint letters in contrasting colors. To make the letters stand out more, go around them with a black marker when the paint is dry.

3. Fix a small magnet on the back of each pebble with white glue.

▶ *Stick your finished pebble letters on the fridge to spell your name or things to remember!*

Instant Pressed Flowers

Cut flowers and leaves don't stay fresh for long, but if you dry them, they last for years. You can sandwich them between heavy books for a few weeks, buy a flower press, or try this super-speedy method.

1. Lay four paper towels on a microwave-proof plate and put a piece of blotting paper on top. Arrange flowers and leaves on the blotting paper.

Make sure they don't overlap.

Dried flowers are delicate, so move them using tweezers.

2. Cover them with another piece of blotting paper and four more paper towels. Put another plate on top to keep everything in place.

3. Put everything in a microwave oven and give 30-second blasts of heat. In total, heat for three or four minutes. Check the flowers every so often—when they're stiff, they're done.

Don't pick wild flowers and leaves without permission! Choose flowers and foliage from bunches of cut flowers or other plants at home.

4. Stick your dried flowers on greeting cards or turn the page to find some more decorative ideas.

Be careful when using a microwave.

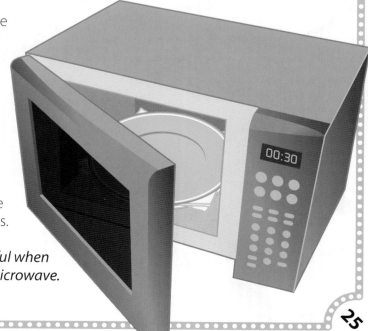

DECORATIVE DETAILS

There are many clever craft techniques to help you personalize photo albums and frames, or liven up homemade cards and containers. Remember not to overdo things. A frame encrusted in colorful materials can distract attention from the photo inside.

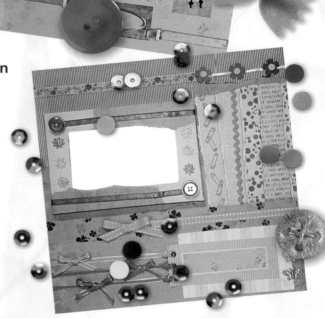

Creative Collage

A great way to decorate the flat surface of a wooden photo frame is with a **collage**. Try using buttons, sequins, beads, yarn, pasta shapes, tissue paper, or patterns cut out from wrapping paper. Stick everything in place with white glue.

▲ *Make your own frames by decorating cardboard and leaving a space for the photo.*

Try making the materials or patterns relevant to the photo in the frame. For example, for a vacation photo, cover a frame in glue, stick on shells and fill in the gaps with sand.

Add a layer of clear varnish to flat collages. It gives a professional finish, and protects your handiwork, too.

Scrapbooking

Scrapbooking involves sticking photos and other bits and pieces into a decorated album. It's a great way to record memories of special events, vacations, or friends. If you don't want to make a whole scrapbook, try designing one page that you can frame.

Start Scrapping

First, decide on a theme—for example, a party you enjoyed. Collect photos, plus souvenirs like tickets, and arrange them on the page. Once you're happy with the layout, stick everything down with glue or photo corner mounts. Add captions or notes and brighten up empty spaces with stickers or patterns.

▲ *Postcards and shells are ideal for decorating a trip scrapbook.*

Decorations stand out if you mount them on larger pieces of card stock in contrasting colors.

Crop photos to focus on important elements.

Best Ever Halloween Party!

Guess who?

This badge glows in the dark

Part of my costume

Invitation to the **Scariest** Party in Town!

Awesome invite!

*Make borders from strips of paper, or use **pinking shears** for a wiggly edge.*

Don't line up everything on the page. Experiment with different angles. Try layering and overlapping.

Think about texture—painted homemade paper (see page 7) can look great.

WHAT NEXT?

The key to developing craft skills is simple—keep doing the things you enjoy! Maybe you love modeling with salt dough or designing puppets. Perhaps you want to try new origami or weaving projects. The more you do, the more skilled you'll become.

Be Inspired

Visit craft shows and museums for inspiration, cut photos from magazines, and jot ideas in a notebook. Collect useful items and keep them in a special box. Experiment with techniques and materials, and don't worry if something doesn't turn out right—it might lead to a better idea.

Expand Your Skills

Try learning other craft skills, such as knitting or sewing. These take time and patience to master, but they allow you to make all kinds of things, including clothes, bags, and toys. Or how about finding local classes teaching jewelry-making, pottery, or woodwork?

▲ Some people use antiques, such as this 200-year-old ring, as inspiration for modern designs.

◄ Knitting isn't as hard as it may look at first. Perhaps someone in your family could teach you?

Further Study

Professional **artisans** begin making things as a hobby, then move on to selling their products once they've developed original ideas. It may help to apply for art or design courses when you leave school. Business skills or website design courses could also help you sell your crafts.

▶ *Artisans often set up market stalls like this one in Tunisia. You could do the same at local fairs.*

Careers in Crafts

A passion for crafts can lead to all kinds of careers. How about designing fashionable hats, shoes, and bags, or props for theater sets, or new products ranging from dinner plates to sports cars? Maybe you could make stained glass windows or carve musical instruments.

◀ ▶ *Who knows where your craft skills will lead? You could create elegant catwalk fashions or make* **clay animation** *characters!*

Improve your designs by practicing art skills like drawing, painting, and printing. Look for another book in this series, Art Skills, for lots of great ideas!

GLOSSARY

acrylic
A fast-drying type of paint, usually sold in tubes. Acrylic paint doesn't wash off when it's dry, so try not to get it on your clothes.

artisan
Another word for a craftsperson, or someone who is skilled at making things by hand.

clay animation
A type of cartoon made using clay figures, which are photographed, then moved slightly, then photographed again, and so on. When the pictures are run together at speed, the clay characters look as if they're moving.

collage
A collection of materials, artistically arranged and glued onto a surface.

crop
To trim so that only the most important or striking parts of a picture remain.

felt
Fabric made of wool or other similar fibers that are pressed together to make a smooth mat of material.

loom
A frame used for weaving. It holds the lengthways threads (called the warp) in place, while the horizontal threads (the weft) are passed under and over from side to side.

marionette
A puppet that has jointed limbs with strings attached, which are worked from above by a puppeteer.

pinking shears
Special scissors with serrated blades that cut in a zigzag pattern.

pulped
Mashed into a soft, wet mass.

watercolor
A type of paint that usually comes in tubes or blocks and is mixed with water. Watercolors work best on paper, but you can also try them on surfaces like wood.

USEFUL WEBSITES

www.activitytv.com
Watch videos or print out instructions for a huge range of craft activities which are helpfully labeled according to skill level. There are lots of categories to choose from at the top of the home page, including crafts, origami, puppets, and jewelry.

www.origami-fun.com/origami-for-kids.htm/
Follow links to instructions for making all kinds of origami animals, flowers, and decorations.

www.papiermache.co.uk
Browse a whole site dedicated to papier-mâché modeling. It includes helpful hints and tips, plus articles about papier-mâché experts and their imaginative creations.

https://nextstep.direct.gov.uk/PlanningYourCareer/JobProfiles/Pages/JobFamily0023.aspx
Find out more about crafty careers, and get lots of practical advice about qualifications, salaries, and job opportunities.

www.carlwarner.com
Get great ideas for food sculptures by looking at artist Carl Warner's weird and wonderful "foodscapes."

INDEX